# What's Stopping you?

## Make that hard decision today!

Selina Davis

# What's Stopping you?

## Make that hard decision today!

Selina Davis

2020 @Nostalgyx LLC

WHAT'S STOPPING YOU?

MAKE THAT HARD DECISION TODAY!

This is a non-fiction book.

Published by @ Nostalgyx LLC

Printed in the United States of America

First Edition December 2020

www.whatstoppingyou.com

ISBN: 978-0-578-81776-7

# DEDICATION

Firstly, I have to thank God for giving me the strength and ability to remain resilient through all my experiences.

I dedicate this book to my mum for always being a constant source of support even when "I" want more. To my husband Eugene, the journey has been challenging but God knows the story His writing and to our amazing children for which I strive daily to demonstrate to always be the best version of themselves.

Leah, Josiah, Joshua, Joel & Keziah not leaving out Brooklyn our dog, Mummy (Mom) loves you.

To my Friends and Family thank you for your support.

Be Blessed

Your greatest breakthrough is one

hard decision away…

SELINA DAVIS

# CONTENTS

# Introduction

————————————

This journey known as life comes with no manual, nor does it look the same for everyone. We live in the moment and we discover ways to maneuver through life figuring it out as we go along.

I never knew a Black English girl from North London (United Kingdom) would have experienced so much in life. Raised predominately by a single mother who endured the experience of physical abuse which she tried to protect us from. My teenage

years were not the highlight of my life as I was
somewhat a nobody but also the popular girls
friend. I did however discover the power of my
body and used that as my way of getting attention
which later lead to some not so nice experiences.
Like most girls and boys growing up with only 1
parent (although I did know my dad, I had a
relationship with him as best as he knew how too)
you tend to feel as if you are lacking something. As
a result of that I was looking for love because I felt
replaced as my dad was having children with other
women at one point whilst still with my mum.

As the lid of sexuality was lifted off when I lost my
virginity so was the many incidences that followed
which resulted in me getting pregnant 3 times of
which two were abortions and one was a
miscarriage. I would like to mention that one of
those abortions was because I actually never knew
who slept with me as all I remember is being on a

11

bench by the side of an apartment block after a house party and was left to be discovered.

Fast forward a few years, God was definitely carrying me as I was introduced to a church by a school mate and it was God, Church and Me. From the age of 21 and a large portion of my young adult life I was dedicated to God and I found my husband and later had 3.5 children during that period. Your probably wondering "0.5" children how possible, well I say that because at the time I was pregnant when we went through what I can call an exodus and the church turned against those that followed Christ and not the pastor (that's deserves a book).

My journey from 2012 onwards is what I called walking on water (Peter style). This is life with no cushion of the church, your foundation being ripped apart and now you have to discover what this life is about on life's terms. This was an experience I will never forget.

Have you ever had to walk into new situations, new territories of life where you really have no clue on earth what you are going to do next? What is life going to look like from here on out. Feeling the level of rejection not only from the church but also from close loved ones and people that you put so much trust in can make you feel lost and unsure.

Whilst I have experienced this and so much more in life as an adult from being a parent to 5 amazing children, getting married, buying my first home, dealing with the effects of generational curses that have lead to alcoholism and drugs in my marriage. Not to mentioned moving thousands of miles away from my hometown of London to the United States of America by pure and utter faith.

There are countless examples that I can provide you with that has led to me making hard life decisions.

13

What has allowed me to stand the test of time, endure all the painful experiences, process my multi-faceted levels and layers of rejection (which, does not stop coming by the way). Meet loneliness even in marriage, fight to hold a family together while standing and holding everything and everyone else around me. What has allowed me to stand, has ultimately been me learning my way through it all. Trusting God even when I turned my back on God. Taking the good, the bad, the emotional whirlwinds, the tears, the happy moments, the lonely and dark moments. One has to find that inner self, that person within that lives and wants better for him or herself.

Had it not been for these experiences and making tuff decisions, I would never have stepped into the ocean to see what faith in action looked like, what making hard decisions meant, what dealing with life-on-life terms would lead me to.

Did I have faith 100% of the time, NO? It took me walking on top of the water to find out. Did I have all the answers? Absolutely not. Who does? But we assume that everyone in and out of our circle or sight or on social media has it all together. I have to believe that my life is and has been laid down in a foundation unknown to me. I know that no matter how low in the pit I have gone, God who takes care of the birds, the plants and the trees, Is the same God that allows no man to control the Sun or Moon by a utility bill. Must have me in His hands. And He has you in His hands too.


Despite it all, I have a firm level of strength and calm about me that I cannot explain.

I am resilient!

I am a fighter!

I am solution minded!

I am determined!

I am a friend!

I am a warrior!

I am a strong black woman

I am a Mom (Mum)


And I am ME and I want you to be YOU.


I know how to trust in God and appreciate his blessings in my life, the journey is just beginning, and I want to bring you along that journey with me. I'm not coming to you as a successful entrepreneur living in her fullest potential. NOT YET but I am coming to you as a real one. Someone that needs to keep my mind on check daily, that needs to keep pushing herself despite how I feel, that understands the hardships of life and all the ups and downs that are involved. I want this to be a book you can relate to now, on your journey to becoming the best version of you and even when you hit your peak of success.

Do you need someone to be accountable to?

Do you need to have a network of strong faithful believing NO Regret warriors?

Life is too short and unpredictable to waste any more time.

We have plenty to achieve and plenty of life to live. So why not start now. But more importantly, start by taking the action steps towards the goals with baby steps not long jumps in marking off hard decisions, one decision at a time.

Understand that what your life looks like to you is different from the next person. This will be a no judgement zone network and relationship. We all deserve to become better and have a better life for ourselves to maximize on what we have to offer and serve with as much as we want to give.

We must be willing to humble ourselves and be real.

Are you ready to tackle the hard decisions head on? Turn the pages of this book and commence the journey.

I believe you have the ability to achieve abundantly above all you can ask or think of through God so just DO IT.

Selina Davis

# 1

# The Pressure Cooker

**(The sound is getting louder)**

The correlation between life and a pressure cooker can be felt when you are in a funnel and you need to make a life altering decision. It's highly stressful and intense much like the sounds coming from a tightly squeezed lid that gets louder and louder.

**Decisions are made once we release that lid and act.**

## The Path

Life has a way of leading you down a path that requires you to make life altering decisions. What decisions am I talking about? You remember listening to your parents complain about things when you were growing up. The mailman better not bring no bad news my way and they look at you like you were meant to know what they were talking about. Or, they ask you questions like *"What is more important? Us having food on the table or you wanting that birthday present?"*. Or *"sorry son or daughter we cannot afford to do that right now as we have other priorities"*. Or *this relationship is really not going anyway but I love him or her.*

Decisions, decisions decisions we hear this so much as kids growing up. Fast forward to being a "young" adult and life hits you with decisions like popcorn popping in the microwave.

*Can you hear it now?*

What tasks should you knock off your to do list?
What bill should you prioritize due to your budget?
Should I go on that first date? How am I going to
juggle taking my kids to school, whilst not having a
car and having to get to work all within 30 mins of
each other. What's for dinner? *I hear you ask.* This has
become like a swear word in my mind (do not ask
me that question, I don't even want to eat food
anymore) ... But for real it's endless and probably
would desire a whole book dedicated to the
different decisions we face.

Here are some of the top 10 decision making events
that occur in our life (no matter who you are):

1.  What career do I want?
2.  What college/university should I attend?
3.  Should I get married or not?
4.  Do I want to have children?

5. Where should I live?

6. Should I buy or rent?

7. What should I do next?

8. What car should I buy?

9. Should I quit smoking or drinking?

10. Should I get back with my ex?

Besides some of these life altering decisions that have become normal and even none-thought provoking at times, there are those life changing decisions that we face that I have come to believe are truly presented to us in order for us to be lead down the path of what some would say is our "Purpose" or "Passion" or life given "Destiny"

Can I just tell you something that happened to me? Life for me was getting extremely tight. I was for a long time feeling like I was missing out on my time with my children as I have been pulled away from them so much over the last few years due to my commitment and employment position at the time.

I juggled being an entrepreneur and employee a number of times as I knew how important my time with the kids was and I needed to find flexibility. It got to a point in my life where 2019 was like hell on earth but no one outside of my walls would have known. I was determined to enter 2020 with a new mindset and my decade mantra of #NOREGRET. Each month I would consciously decide to change something in my life and then March hit and I knew it was time to handle my job as everything around me was becoming a strain. Therefore, not being able to commit to this full-time job was the only way forward for me. From all angles things were getting so tight and I felt was just causing things to move in this direction. I can only explain it like a funnel that I was literally being piped out of and now I was approaching the bottom. I needed flexibility, I needed to spend more time at home, I needed to make the sacrifice for my husband to get out of the house and back to work and I wanted to be home.

This decision didn't come lightly as I was leaving my 6-figure corporate job and lifestyle to land back to ground zero.

Yes 6-figures sounds great but when you divide that among my 5 children, living expenses, no personal help outside of myself and my husband and at the time we couldn't afford childcare then yes that doesn't stretch very far.

It was my time to also allow my husband and father of my children to start getting himself out there as he was holding it down at home. Which if I'm at all honest had been causing a lot of personal issues and a huge strain on our relationship and THEN COVID-19 hit the world and what was "normal" was now all changing right before our eyes.

**THE STREAM**

God gives us signs and when I had made my decision to resign 3 days prior to the news that schools were shutting down, no one that traveled via public transportation could come into the office then all these signs were just confirmations that God was and is truly in control. Please note I had no idea of what was to come next, I just knew I had to listen.

Decisions, decisions, decisions now is the time. I know deep down in my heart God needs you to sacrifice and trust in him and everything will align with the signs. I know my example in this context is relating to work but yours maybe to start a fresh new life (I did that too back in 2015), or check into that rehab clinic to finally clean up your life or leave that relationship or simply to start taking care of yourself for once. Whatever the decision is; be it big or small, it's time to take the pressure cooker lid off and take the leap of faith to get started.

*Trust God from the bottom of your heart; don't*

*try to figure out everything on your own.
Listen for God's voice in everything you do,
everywhere you go; he's the one who will keep
you on track. Don't assume that you know it
all. Proverbs 3:3-5 MSG*

We don't get anywhere if we're not willing to
remove the voice of doubt and trust in the process.

What decisions are you facing RIGHT now that
requires the lid to be taken off?

_____

_____

_____

From the above what's stopping you?

_____

_____

_____

_____

What can you do NOW as a step towards releasing

that pressure lid?

_____

_____

_____

_____

*I believe it's the decisions we make now that will result in*
*the destination we land in tomorrow. Why wait as time*
*waits for no man so you are only wasting your own time.*

27

# 2

# The Leap

**(Take the steps)**

So, you think you're ready to fly and take the steps
needed at this junction in life?

I commend and encourage you to go for it, you will
see that you wished you had done this ages ago.

Wow, what an amazing feeling to actually action
and release all that pressure. It must feel like you're
flying in the air (not that I personally know what
flying in the air feels like) but hey that's the beauty
of visualization.

For me it felt right, I knew it was my time, I knew I

had to make the move that I did for the betterment of my family but ultimately for me. What was I waiting for, everything had aligned itself for such a time and I'm thankful for actually doing it. Now let me just reel this back some as you at this point may still be at the cusp, on the ledge not quite ready to let go and let God.

*Can I ask you a question?*

If this decision were to vanish and you remained in the same situation you are in right now. Would you be happy?

Imagine if nothing changes will you be living the best version of yourself? If the answer is YES, then perhaps this isn't the time for change BUT if the answers is a clear NO then the only person who will regret not taking that step will be you.

For me I replayed the situation out in my mind and

said to myself if in a years' time from now will being here be something I will be proud of? Depending on what that answer was should determine what action you need to take.

## IT'S TIME TO FLY

Taking this leap of faith instantly allowed me more time with my family and being a mother. I was constantly away from them due to the nature of my work plus I had seriously sacrificed a lot for my job which had played a major strain on my home life. Speaking to anyone that is single, married, a parent, an entrepreneur or a career chaser there will be things in your life that is creating physical, mental and emotional strains and at some point you need to ensure you are balancing out what is important to you. Remember that life can never truly be balanced (work/life balance) but recently I listened to Tiffany "Budgetnista" Aliche and she said work life balance isn't possible BUT creating harmony is. What you do in life should work in harmony with each other. MIC DROP! (thank her later).

Are you ready now for the rug to be pulled from underneath you? That feeling is going to feel somewhat unnerving or uncomfortable whatever your decision is surrounding. Whether it's a financial change, relationship change, or a personal development change you won't know what's next until you make those moves.

I do want to state this, that change does not directly come with an instant reward all the time. It will take you going through the change to gain the rewards and also it may not look the way you anticipate it to look. What I want you to do though, is embrace the journey from here on out and buckle up for the ride.

Stepping out in faith yields tremendous rewards

31

but you must be in it for the long haul.

*"To live, to TRULY live, we must be willing to take a RISK. To be nothing in order to find everything. To leap before we look."*

Do this breathing exercise: Whilst sitting with your palms facing up. Inhale and expand your diaphragm outward for 2-3 secs and exhale and return your abdomen to its normal position. Repeat 3-5 times.

How are you feeling right now?

_____

_____

_____

_____

If you are still toiling or feeling indecisive with the
idea of making that decision – be honest with
yourself and write your answer down to that
question on page 24.

_____

_____

_____

_____

_____

_____

What actions can you take to overcome 1 or 2 of the
items you have placed above?

_____

_____

_____

_____

_____

*If all you have is yourself, I want you to start trusting in YOU and believing in who you are...*

# 3

# The Silence

## (The freedom)

You can breathe; *No* nothing is wrong; you don't
have to worry that feeling your feeling right now is
what the other side of making a decision feels like.
The burden you have been carrying has been lifted
off your shoulders.

Now assuming you have taken that leap of faith to
making that decision this is essentially Day 1.

You may be feeling a number of emotions right now
but what I want you to do is take a moment and

place your feet flat on the ground, *go on* move off the bed or position yourself correctly on that chair. With your feet flat on the ground take a deep breath… INHALE, EXHALE, repeat this 3 times and sit for a few minutes in silence.

What is your mind speaking to you right now? Write it down – *if you need more space get a piece of paper.*

_____

_____

_____

_____

_____

_____

_____

_____

_____

You may not know what tomorrow has in store but I want you to be still in this moment and really celebrate this small or big win depending on the level of decision making you have had to make, reflect on where you are right now.

This was a surreal experience for me, for the first time in such a long time I did not have to answer to a demand or an email or a phone call at that moment in time. I literally took this moment to shed myself from the burden I was carrying for so long. I am a super loyal individual so when I'm committed to something, I'm all in. This unfortunately has led me to experience some very personal and devastatingly disappointing situations, as I placed my value and reliance on what other people wanted from me rather than what I wanted for myself. I am learning that what we have to offer or give to the world should first start with us valuing ourselves. Yes, we must first see that we are an asset not a liability and that when we put our greatness out there, we must understand that people will take it in different ways. That feeling of relief, the relaxed shoulders, the calm emotion and the ability to even take in this moment shouldn't be ignored. You must allow yourself this moment with no apologies, no worries or no shadow of doubt.

## FREEDOMVILLE

Your mind maybe going a million miles per hour right now. The essence of even being quiet maybe even hard for you to take in as you have never given yourself this kind of time.

I call this moment freedomville, which is the moment or moments when you literally don't think of anything outside of the sound of silence. Take some time today and go outside, sit on your driveway or take a stroll. I mean literally right now put this book down and GO.

I want to say I'm proud of you, even if this is a small step towards making the bigger decisions...

CONGRATULATIONS.

We tend to only think big wins are worth celebrating but in fact it's the smaller wins along the journey to the big ones that yield the everlasting moments of change. You should embrace this time and don't take it lightly. For some this has been years in the making, months of deliberation, days of contemplating and hours and hours of self-mind talk and conversations.

*Even if I knew that tomorrow the world would go to pieces, I would still plant my apple tree.*

*Martin Luther*

To many times we don't action things in fear of the unknown, but we must learn to sow the seeds for change to occur.

Write down 3 things you are grateful for?

1.




2.




3.

How do you feel right now?

_____

_____

_____

_____

_____

_____

_____

What about this moment do you wish to hold onto?

_____

_____

_____

_____

_____

_____

Remember this change or action can be repeated over and over again as we face decisions constantly. I want you to remember the feeling you feel as this will encourage you for the next time even if those feelings are uncomfortable change doesn't always feel good in the moment.

# 4

# The Energy

## (Energizer bunny reborn)

Like an energizer bunny you're off or perhaps the sound of the gun master at a relay race just went off. Where should you start? So many things to do and you have the feeling that you can conquer the world.

You may be saying to yourself why didn't I make these changes ages ago? This newfound freedom your experiencing stepping into the unknown or beginning a fresh new start can feel surreal. Whether it means rolling on your bed in peace or starting your day with a clear mind or not clocking into a 9-5 you will have a sense of renewing.

This for me was epic although I have been here before it still feels different. My mindset was evolving, and I was growing in my perspective of life in this moment. *There is so much I want to organize; my creative juices are flowing. I want to build my knowledge and read books, look up aspirational people to watch and learn from, profiles to update, posts to post, OMG my house can FINALLY get cleaned.* The message I was hearing was you have the time now to plan your day the way you want it to go.

Time has not stopped but finally I can appreciate the 24hrs in my day and actually enjoy the outside. Living surrounded by so many trees, the wildlife running around my garden, my kids can finally say, "Are you working at home today? YES, and they are so happy to have me present. That feeling is priceless.

Your decision may be pertaining to a relationship

either intimate or a friendship, it could have been a business partnership that went left. It could have been the decision to finally get your health sorted out and now you can start that treatment plan or it could have been the decision to finally put yourself first and you can now do the things you have been putting off for years or months. Whatever your decision was in this moment flow with that energy see what you can accomplish but remember not to replace what you may have removed with something else as a filler.

It's unreal how much energy we put into people, situations or negative thought patterns that have held us hostage for so long. I didn't realize how much I was talking myself out of making decisions until I became aware of them. I know your energy maybe at 100% right now so I want you to during this process become more aware of your thoughts and feelings.

# Why?

The more I became aware of the thoughts that were speaking to me and holding me back, the quicker I have become in stopping them from fully taking me backwards. It's also very important that you start to consciously make an effort in removing the untruths that you have been speaking to yourself over the years. These have become norms in your subconscious mind which has dominated the way in which you think and makes what should be easy decisions much harder to make.

There are no time limits set on how long you will be feeling this sense of freedom. It may last 24hrs, 3 days, a week or longer. It really depends on the level of change you have just done or the impact of what that decision has on your life. Regardless of the time I want you to really start re-writing what your future will look like from hence forward.

> Yesterday's the past, tomorrow's the
> future, but today is a gift. That's why it's
> called the present.
> Bil Keane

Exercise:

For the next 7 Days I want you to write the following below at the top of a piece of a paper (Over the summer this was an activity that I completed as it really changed the way I see things and put things into prospective).

Write: WHAT I REALLY WANT IS…... (from this sentence starter you will just write for about 10/15 mins. Don't think about what your about to write or the grammatical errors, just let the words flow on the page). Once complete do not read what you have written for the next 7 days. Repeat this exercise **every day** for 5 more days and on day 7 is when you will re-read each page paying attention to the areas within your writing that have repetition.

This my friend is your next step to living your life with #NOREGRET

Turn on some motivational music or relaxation instrumental so that you can get into the zone.

Use the following pages per day or you can use a notebook.

# WHAT'S STOPPING YOU? MAKE THAT HARD DECISION TODAY?

Day 1:

_____

_____

_____

_____

_____

_____

_____

_____

_____

_____

_____

_____

_____

_____

_____

_____

_____

_____

_____

Day 2:

_____

_____

_____

_____

_____

_____

_____

_____

_____

_____

_____

_____

_____

_____

_____

_____

_____

_____

_____

Day 3:

_____

_____

_____

_____

_____

_____

_____

_____

_____

_____

_____

_____

_____

_____

_____

_____

_____

_____

_____

Day 4:

_____

_____

_____

_____

_____

_____

_____

_____

_____

_____

_____

_____

_____

_____

_____

_____

_____

_____

_____

WHAT'S STOPPING YOU? MAKE THAT HARD DECISION
TODAY?

Day 5:

_____

_____

_____

_____

_____

_____

_____

_____

_____

_____

_____

_____

_____

_____

_____

_____

_____

_____

---

---

---

---

---

---

---

---

---

---

---

---

---

---

---

---

---

---

---

---

Day 6:

_____

_____

_____

_____

_____

_____

_____

_____

_____

_____

_____

_____

_____

_____

_____

_____

_____

_____

Day 7:

You will now re-read each day and highlight anything that has been repeated over the course of the 6 days. Below put the top 3 things that were a repetition.

Write your key findings here:

1)_____

_____

_____

2)_____

_____

_____

3)_____

_____

_____

How are you feeling right now?

_____

_____

_____

_____

_____

_____

_____

You're a champion, and you need to say that to yourself. For anyone to get the best in you, you must first see the best in yourself and believe in you.

# 5

# The Mind Games

**(Where are these thoughts coming from)**

Doesn't freedomville feel good however life prior
to the change hasn't changed fully. Now I'm
starting to get those thoughts in my head that's
making me look back at that decision. Can I
possibly go back? Did I make the right choice?
Why are the feelings coming to me?

Life is sweet and things are starting to come together
until you start to notice that old thoughts are trying
to resurface and bring back memories of things that
once were. This is real and these are the moments we

spoke about taking control of as these are your comfort zone triggers, those self-talking conversations that you have with yourself.

For me, the reality of my freedomville honeymoon was passing over sooner than I wanted it to and now I have to make an even more conscious decision about my thoughts and what actions I take with them.

Change is effective when you start to take the actions needed and implement that into all areas of your life.

I remember when I started thinking about the practical things, I was responsible for. You know going from a 6-figure salary to ground zero is a very hard decision to make especially when you do not have a safety net (another job to fall back on). Not only was I establishing a NEW business in an economic crisis, but I was also becoming an at home teacher to 5 children each in different grades as the world was shutting down at the exact same time. The basic necessities of life didn't take those things into consideration instantly. The bills, the need to eat, the need to have a roof over your head and the list goes on. This is probably classic occurrences for anyone whose decision was sentenced around the reduction of income.

.......... *Ring ring, ring ring*

**Operator:** "Hello, it's said company calling as your account is behind in payment"

**Me:** "Okay, well I don't have it at the moment"

**Operator:** "When can you make a payment?"

**Me:** "Well to be honest I don't know but can you defer my payment"

**Operator:** "No, unfortunately we can't so your service won't be restored until the full payment is paid in full"

**Me:** "But, I have 5 kids at home what am I supposed

to do"

**Operator:** "Unfortunately, there isn't anything we can do at this point until its paid"

**Me:** "Okay what's the latest date you can provide me, and I'll take that"

**Operator:** "Okay, is there anything else I can help you with?

**Me:** "No, as you haven't helped me at all on this call so thank you"

**Operator:** "Okay, sorry and you have a great rest of your day", "Please stay on the line to complete our survey"

**Me:** CLICK


This continued with everything imaginable until the day came. The lights went out and we were without electricity, internet (mind you we were still in e-learning mode) and the water was attached to the septic tank which is attached to electricity so that was off also. Not forgetting my phone was cut off at this point so I was relying on internet calls via WhatsApp and Facebook.

### What are we going to do?

We stood in the kitchen and was like is that the electric for real for real!!

If this has ever happened to you, the sound of your electricity getting switched off from the main line is not the same as a power cut. I knew and felt it in my gut, as we have had plenty of power cuts before. I stayed there for what may have only been a few minutes or even more but then my mind started doing what it does best, what can I do to get us out of this situation.

Going straight to my office desk checking all my accounts from app to app I closed each one knowing that there was nothing available for me to even attempt to get this sorted. At this point it was full payment or nothing. I sat there looking at my kids, thinking about the day and time of which was mid-afternoon, and it would soon be dark.

We all went outside at that point and started enjoying nature as I needed to connect and destress my thoughts and calm any panic as I could not control anything in that moment. I recognized that and knew it benefitted me not to worry or stress out but to just trust that God would work this all out.

You know what's amazing about kids, is that they are resilient and so adaptable. When we came back in the house, they started building a fort and then we started locating the flashlights and making sure they all worked. By then we wanted to also make sure that we had charged phones or device but of course that wasn't happening apart from in the car. Oh, did I tell you it was teacher parents conference starting that evening and we had nothing on. Thank God my laptop was on charge prior. We were able to scrap the Wi-Fi hotspot but minutes to my last conference call my laptop battery died, and the house got dark. It was night, we ordered pizza and had a camp night with all the flashlights on in the bedroom.

We sat together for the first time in months eating and talking until we knocked out and went to bed.


## WHAT ARE YOU MADE OF?


I'm sure you have had to endure some moments in your life where you may have felt stripped, all the way back and things felt out of your control. Can you recall how it made you feel in that moment? What was your response to that situation? You see sometimes, unless we go through things, we will never know how we will handle a situation. We don't even realize that we have the ability to overcome so much but it's because of these moments and circumstances that shake and turn what we deem as a "comfortable life" or "our comfort zone".

69

Only then do we come to those realizations. Do we have to suffer or get hurt or experience a loss for us to see what we are made of. The answer is not really BUT and it's a big but why, because we tend to be hard headed and don't always learn the lessons even when the situation appears right as we tend to take things for granted so it shows up in other areas.

> *"For God has not given us a spirit of fear and timidity, but of power, love, and self-discipline".*
> *2 Timothy 1:7 NLT*

What thoughts are coming into your mind right now?

_____

_____

_____

_____

_____

Can you identify situations in your life where you lost all control? Highlight up to 3 of them below.

1)_____

_____

2)_____

_____

3)_____

_____

Choice 1 of the above and write down how you dealt with that situation?

_____

_____

_____

_____

How would you perhaps approach it again should something similar happen out of your control?

_____

_____

_____

_____

_____

_____

_____

_____

Our minds are like a revolving think tank that will constantly keep going until we retrain it to be fluid with the right thoughts to move us forward. Remember we won't always be in control so work on things that allow you to deal with those moments to control what you are able to and give what you can't to God.

# 6

# The Slope

## (The reality)

Face your reality head on, do not be ashamed of where you are right now. Do not hide your reality from yourself as it doesn't benefit you in the long run. The biggest lie we can tell ourselves is living out the lies we convince ourselves to be true.

It's not easy, you may experience loneliness, you may face anxiety, your support system may have gone, the love of your life may no longer be around and you have to wake up dealing with life on life's terms.

Reality looks different when you take the leap of faith to make the changes needed in your life.

Whether you make those changes or life caused you to make those changes, you will have to face your reality head on.

## WHERE TO GO FROM HERE?

Are you having to discover a new life? A new way of thinking and feeling? A new way of supporting yourself. And or are you now really having to trust and rely on God. Whilst I knew that my recent decisions in life were caused by God pushing and pressing on me to make the changes, I also knew that there was going to be challenges that would drastically affect our lives. We were going from 10 to 0 real quick and I couldn't put my trust in anyone other than trusting God to make a way. Now trust and our reality doesn't always match up. It doesn't mean those bills will stop as I mentioned in chapter 5, doesn't mean that your ex won't attempt to call you or plead to have you back, doesn't mean you won't see your colleague in that new role because you didn't apply for that job. Now that last sentence may have you thinking!!! Yes, I said it – you may be looking at your colleague in that new position because you failed to apply for it. Trust and believe that making NO decision is just like making THE decision. If you don't make a decision, there are consequences that will likely affect you as well as if you do make the right decision. A decision is a decision.

What it highlighted to me this time around in my life is that I needed to look at my reality differently. I needed to now look from a different set of lenses but what did that mean as I had not seen anything other than what my life was at that point.

What I decided to do was go and find out how to expand my mind, how to think bigger and find people that were living life in a way I was not accustomed too. Did I have them in my immediate circle? the answer was no, so I had to go and find them. Read about them, listen to them, feed my spirit with what God had said about my life and what he had done for others. I knew my reality now was just that, my reality in this moment only and not one that was going to project into my thoughts and actions for my tomorrow.

When your life is being ordered by God, he would have caused you to make that decision perhaps not in the most ideal scenario. Well at least for me it helped my understanding that no matter how hard my reality was getting how low or deep my feelings were going. I had to dig deep in my relationship with God. Within this journey I have come to see what foundation I have underneath me. Where I place my trust and what shakes that foundation. It's not easy, nor is it all sunshine and roses. However, what I can tell you is that my greatest strength has for the most part come from my lowest and weakest moments.

We all think about the downward motion of a slope and how steep it is. When looking from the top of a mountain our vision to the end is limited and at best we can anticipate when it will end but we do not really know. What I can tell you is that the only way to find out is by going through that motion and feeling every element of the experience to identify where you are.

## YOU CAN DO THIS...

How do you deal with your emotions in this situation? How are you coping through the unknown? What and who are you trusting in? Who do you have as a support system?

What comes with facing your reality and looking at the slope head on is where you will realize your true self. Who you really are at the core will show itself up! Grow to either love what you discover or learn to embrace what may be unfamiliar so you can start to truly love you. Just be open and willing to start the journey.

For I know the plans I have for you," says the Lord. "They are plans for good and not for disaster, to give you a future and a hope.

Jeremiah 29:11

What are you discovering about yourself?

_____

_____

_____

What are you going to embrace and work on?

_____

_____

_____

Write down one thing that you're grateful for right
now?

-------------------------------------------------------------------

-------------------------------------------------------------------

-------------------------------------------------------------------

Don't over think this process and don't stress
yourself out trying to figure each intricate step. You
will get your groove on eventually this is part of the
journey.

# 7

# The Emotions

**(The ups & the downs)**

Wow, what your discovering about yourself from your emotions is powerful. We have been told that our emotions are bad, especially when referring to the "bad ones" such as anger, frustration and rage.

What if I told you that, that wasn't the truth?

What if your perspective on these words were mainly linked to past experiences and not really the true definition lived out?

For example, let's look at the word "Frustration":

Defined: *the feeling of being upset or annoyed, especially because of* **inability to change** *or* **achieve something** / *the prevention of the progress, success, or fulfillment of something.*

Looking closely at this emotion or feeling we so often get. We can clearly see that its linked to our inability to change something, act or gain clarity to make the decisions we need which then leads to us getting frustrated. What if you would turn that frustration into action? How long do you think you will be frustrated for if you applied this every time you were in that emotion?

Worth thinking about!

## FAST AND FURIOUS 101

Our emotions are amazing assets that mankind possesses. It connects us to our inner being and others including how we deal with life through them. My "passion" which really is my anger for a situation had led me to feel so angry that not only did I get the emotional high of anger, but what I felt was happening is that it was breaking a part of me that turned that anger into realized passion. This experience has happened over a period of situations and stages before I recognized it in this way. Let me break it down:

**Stage 1**: Initial blindsided anger directly to the person or situation.

**Stage 2**: Reasoning as to why I was justified to feel that way.

**Stage 3**: Speaking to myself as if that person were in front of me.

**Stage 4**: Prayer kicked in (Deep *deep* prayer)

**Stage 5**: Compassion for others who have been victims to this same treatment.

**Stage 6:** My anger now became my fuel to my passion that I must do what I can to make people not feel the emotional turmoil of such insecure people. But more importantly help people to not feel insecure when receiving such treatment.

My passionate anger converted itself to my purpose. It was showing me that what I was getting frustrated and even angry about was in fact stirring up what was already inside of me. If I'm honest this has happened to me before around the same kind of incidence. You may have never looked at it from this perspective before but if you take a minute right now and reflect on a situation or a series of situations that have led you to be extremely upset, frustrated or even angry. Do you see any similarities in the outcome of how you have reacted to that situation? Let me give this example: I was informed of an opinion made about me from someone. I also read how they valued me and what arose inside, was a deep level of passion and anger towards the audacity of that person. Some would say it was the Holy Spirit, or inner self connecting to the fact that a position had led someone to forget where they came from which displayed to me a level of arrogance that was unacceptable. What made it even more intense in that moment was that my feelings were not just about me. It was about the value that we placed on others and how we can get so high in positions, prestige and status that we belittle people and have the nerve to speak it. That day I felt a reminder from God, that my spirit connected too. My passion for others and how we as individuals need to truly get to a place within ourselves that doesn't place our value in the hands of another human being. We must work on valuing ourselves first and lay that foundation right.

**PUMP THE BREAKS...**

As you can see the emotions we deem to be "bad" when fully understood or explored at a time in your life when you are open for growth are in fact not at all bad rather an enlightening experience of growth.

Now you may be thinking yeh right this *ain't me no way*. There is no way my anger or frustration or any emotion in that regard can become my passion or purpose. I truly believe that what we get the most passionate about especially in the area of frustration or anger means we have a part to play in changing it or helping others change it.

In this context, I want you to consciously make a decision right now and challenge yourself to firstly be open, be willing to grow and take the time to explore the deeper feelings, even when you are confronted.

We all want the happy, joyful, peaceful emotions to land in our lives daily. Remember even those emotions aren't truly lived out in its true form either. They tend to be situational or circumstantial. We must be willing and open to make daily choices to welcome them into our lives and explore the deeper meanings that allow us to live in that way.

*Don't let your emotions distract you from doing what needs to be done. Control your emotions so your emotions do not control you.*
*Unknown*

Are you willing to explore what your "bad" emotions can reveal?

_____

_____

_____

_____

Can you honestly say that you want these emotions to remain linked to experiences you did not consciously assign them to?

_____

_____

_____

What 3 things will you allow yourself to do when these emotions arise so you can gain a difference outcome?

1._____

2._____

3._____

Feel empowered to allow your emotions to reveal themselves to you but do not allow your emotions to control you. Take stock, take control and take a fresh new outlook on them ALL.

# 8

# The Calm

**(Letting go)**

With every storm you may hit trenches and the terrain. Before you get overwhelmed and anxious by everything, STOP for a minute... Think and reflect on other occasions in your life that you have experienced this storm. Observe how you dealt with it. Proceed as you overcome.

What normally follows a bad storm is the calm.

It's the let go and let God which really means the giving up of your will and want to control everything.

88

## RELEASE THE KITE

Life is truly a series of events that lead to a series of decision-making experiences. Some will last longer than others and some may bind itself into the sequel. My experience has shown me that this period when you let go produces calm. The moment I let go and stopped trying to do things my own way, a sense of peace, assurance and calm came over me. When I look at the situation or circumstances head on, I'm learning to release my need to have the answer to everything especially if I'm honest with myself in knowing I can't control anything in that moment.

It's taken me some time to get to that place of calm after a storm. If I don't catch myself quick enough there go I venting my feelings and talking to myself with these heated conversations as if I was in court winning a case.

I'm sounding the ALARM, **WAKE UP**. Time is going and you realize your either getting tired of repeating the situation or even worst the other person has no clue that you feel this way and has moved on with their life.

Don't allow the situation to hold you captive. You made the right decision or at least stepped towards your decision so don't look back.

Stand firm with your decision, release the tension and let go.

What do I mean by the calm stage, it's the stillness, it's reflecting on the now moment, and self-evaluation on where you want to go from here? It is the action steps and the conviction that *you got this*. Now by the grace of God you can move forward knowing, it can only get better from here. Some useful things that worked for me was creating new habits, such as waking up early every morning. Now that took me some time and actually, I was challenged to be accountable to my coach to actually create that harmony needed in my life to achieve that goal. As I have always put other people first, I have started doing things for myself without guilt (and I'm still learning to do this). Yours may not be waking up early, yours could be walking more, or maybe eating healthier, learning how to better communicate with those that are close to you. Whatever that looks like for you be consistent, be intentional, be more forgiving of yourself and ultimately really learn to appreciate and be grateful for the journey you're on.

Do whatever it takes before the hustle and bustle of the day, start putting more structure into your life, start spending more time with the ones you love and really start doing what is right for your life.

I want to say this, your flow of life may change, and things don't always go to plan. Your perceived perceptions for what you want life to look like may not be there right now. What I know for sure is that if you constantly make the steps toward change, invest in improving yourself, create stability in your thoughts and expand on dreams and visions you will definitely be on the path towards a lasting and evolving change.

> He calms the storm,
> So that its waves are still
> Psalm 107:29

What does calm look like to you?

1._____

_____

2._____

_____

3._____

_____

Choose one of the above and write down how you
will protect this over the next 7 days.

_____

_____

_____

_____

_____

_____

How did it go. Were you able to hold true to it? If
yes, you can now move to the next one. If not, why?

_____

_____

_____

_____

_____

_____

_____

_____

Trust and believe that the footsteps you create must be your own. Don't look to walk anyone else's steps as your journey deserves to be that just yours.

# 9

# The Resilience

(The confident assurance)

The essence of life really boils down to a series of moments that we discover which aids us through the journey. Once you grasp that motion you will be equipped to transition through these moments much easier.

Countless times we defer making some of the hardest decisions for so many reasons; fear of failing, fear of the unknown, or you don't trust yourself to be fully committed in that decision.

Whatever that thing or reason is that has or had prevented you from making that leap to create a new journey for yourself. I want you to reflect on how not making that change will play out in your life.

What does another year or even five years look like in the same situation? *God says that we should trust in the Lord with of all our heart and lean not unto our own understanding. But in all our ways we should acknowledge him, and He will direct your path.*

## FAIL FORWARD

I want to bring you to an experience that happens to us when we are babies. Before you walked you created your own style of crawling, you established that moving your knees or wobbling on your belly or sitting down and moving on the floor like a snake was your way of getting from one area to another. This was further enforced as you had cheerleaders celebrating your success with every movement. Your mom or dad or guardian would have encouraged you to make the first step, *"come on, come on you can do it"*. At the time I wonder what was processing in our minds as we had no clue what we were doing. Perhaps worry kicked in, perhaps uncertainty rose its head or perhaps the feeling of failing or just perhaps we thought nothing. All you knew in that moment is that you needed to make it into the hands of your parents/guardians as they outstretched their arms.

You made the first step and perhaps two, and then you fell down. More than likely you got back up with the reassurance of your care-giver either congratulating you in the excitement and you felt empowered to do it again and again and again.

Today you may never have looked back at that moment in your life or nor did you really know what to expect from that outcome, you just knew it was time to walk. You are there again today at that junction in life when you just need or needed to do it! YES WALK. Whether it was a conscious decision or unconscious one you have to trust in the process and be still and content in knowing that it is well.

You will get through this; you will land back on your feet. Your emotions may be shaking right now, you may even have a nervousness about you, but can I tell you something? The same way that you were determined to take your first step that's the same action you need as you read these pages.

I want you to pull that out of yourself again, not allowing life and all its heavy experiences stop you from trusting God. God has caught you in the past, he will catch you in the present and he will definitely guide you in the future.

You have and can do this…

If you don't like something change it.  If
you can't change it, change your attitude
about it.

Maya Angelou

What are you feeling at this moment?

_____

_____

_____

_____

What may be stopping you from trusting in God?

_____

_____

_____

_____

What have you overcome in your past that seemed impossible at the time?

_____

_____

_____

_____

_____

You are able to make effective change only if you are able to see that change is possible.

Be still and know that God's got your back and will be with you. But ultimately you have to believe in you.

# 10

# The Marathon

## (The journey continues)

We must learn to understand that one decision made will lead to others that need to be made. Whether big or small. We either face them head on, or we go around them like a plague, only to find that they pop their heads up in other areas of repeat reoccurrence.

## THE SKYS THE LIMIT

The unknown can be hard for us to comprehend or face but taking the time to stand in the moment, embrace a new direction, a new feeling, a new adventure that lies ahead can provide a better prospective and a clear outlook on that situation.

I myself am like you in many ways. I don't have all the answers, nor do I have an action plan from the jump. What I believe is common to us both is that we do want to embrace the change and realize our growth potential as we have lived life far too long to not want the best for ourselves. Regardless of age.

Do I know if I will be comfortable with the next steps? Do I want to feel emotions of uncertainty? I would answer that as no, but ultimately, I would say that it hasn't done my life wrong by following and embracing that feeling and taking actions needed for change.

Can I help you out with something little...?

Can I ask that you open your heart and expand the limitations you place on yourself?

Don't doubt yourself so much, stop comparing your life and its direction by the ideals of family and friends or by social media or even by the notion that everything has to be perfect.

Look that was me. I was so guilty of putting the feelings and opinions of others before myself. I was living in a limited bubble although my life was progressing. I did not want to show or share all that I was doing because I did not want my shine to outshine others. I did not want people to look into my life and judge it as being perfect. Unfortunately, social media has become a vicious place that people judge people with no context of the journey you are on or what you are facing or having to overcome just to be present in that day. Your journey is just that yours so learn to appreciate what that's going to look like for you. Ask yourself these honest questions that will help you get unstuck and start to live life fuller. The biggest lessons I have learnt and heard from so many people is that the worst life is not that you have had the trials and tribulations but one that was filled with regrets. One where you wished you would have done this, or did that, or you put it off, brushed it under the carpet or just learnt to live with it. I believe if you are reading this book or message from my heart that you truly want to live a true and authentic life that you can be proud of. As you make the steps needed to embrace the series of decision-making events one decision at a time, don't overwhelm yourself with having to have all the answers, or the blueprint of what's next.

Just follow these steps, which is the acronym STOP:

**S** – Stop waiting for others to change, just start.

**T** – Think about what this is doing to your life.

**O** – Observe if you want to be in this situation.

**P** – Proceed with the steps and actions needed.

Trust in the Lord with all your heart;
do not depend on your own
understanding.
Seek his will in all you do,
and he will show you which path to take.
Proverbs 3:3-5

You're one step closer to change and if you have changed situations in your life during this time of reading congratulations. I'm proud of you and can't wait to hear your amazing stories. But if you have not quite made a tiny step forward, I believe you are almost there. Use this as a guide to help ask yourself those tuff questions so you can make the changes needed for you.

# STAY CONNECTED

Selina Davis, born and raised in London has been on an interesting journey of life thus far and sees that her purpose is to help others much like herself. She believes we seek validation from others and when we do not get it or receive what we are looking for from those around us, disappointment sets in.

We must first start by laying out who we are and work on seeing ourselves the way we want to see us. We are better together when we are honest and willing to work on our inner beings.

Be sure to connect with me on

www.whatstoppingyou.com

Instagram & Facebook @selinacdavis

Sign up as resources will be made available to you.

Follow the podcast Butt-Naked Wisdom available
on all platforms.

Look forward to taking this ride with you and
hearing all your stories and feedback.

Please share on Social media and tag me in I would
love to see you all.

# WHAT'S STOPPING YOU? MAKE THAT HARD DECISION TODAY?

www.ingramcontent.com/pod-product-compliance
Lightning Source LLC
La Vergne TN
LVHW011336080426
835513LV00006B/377